TOGETHER IN MINISTRY EVERYDAY
Workbook

Other Resources for
Together in Ministry Everyday

T.I.M.E. Workbook (9780687653287)
T.I.M.E. 52 Devotions (9780687653683)
T.I.M.E. DVD (9780687653485)
T.I.M.E. Planning Kit (9780687653584)

time

TOGETHER IN MINISTRY EVERYDAY

Workbook

LORI CRANTFORD

Abingdon Press
Nashville

TOGETHER IN MINISTRY EVERYDAY: Workbook

This book is printed on acid-free, recycled paper.

08 09 10 11 12 13 14 15 16 17 – 10 9 8 7 6 5 4 3 2 1

MANUFACTURED IN THE UNITED STATES OF AMERICA

Contents

Go Fish! Series

"As Jesus walked by the Sea of Galilee, he saw two brothers, Simon, who is called Peter, and Andrew his brother, casting a net into the sea—for they were fishermen. And he said to them 'Follow me and I will make you fish for people.' Immediately, they left their nets and followed him."

Matthew 4:18-20

The GO FISH! game consists of 40 playing cards with different types of brightly colored fish (pink, red, orange, purple, brown, green, blue, yellow, white, or gray) on each individual card. The goal is to get a set of four cards of the same color of fish and lay them down in front of you. The person who gets the most sets of same-colored fish is the winner of the game.

A player will ask other players if they have a certain color fish card in their hand and if they do, they have to surrender it to the person requesting it. If they don't have it they will say GO FISH! and the player requesting the card will have to draw a card from the central stack.

Many young children love to play this game, and I have played it for hours with my young grandchildren. The principle of the game is simple. If you cannot get the card you need from another player you have to GO FISH! which means you have to reach out and hope to draw the card you need. The GO FISH! Series is about encouraging followers of Jesus to "GO FISH," which means to reach out to the people in their communities in compassionate, loving ways so that people without any current interest in following Jesus might want to come and become a part of a particular faith community.

Jesus practiced the same principle when he called the brothers Peter and Andrew to become his first followers. Peter and Andrew were fishermen on the sea of Galilee, which means that they would get in their boat each day, go out to the deep part of the lake, throw out their nets, and hopefully pull in a catch of fish.

Peter and Andrew did not sit in their boat near the shore and wait for the fish to come and jump into their boat. They knew that they had to go out to the deep water in order to catch the fish and bring them into their boat. They had to reach out to catch the fish; the fish wouldn't automatically come to them. They had to GO FISH!

In a similar way, congregations need to go out into their neighborhoods and communities in loving and serving ways if they want to invite more persons to become followers of Jesus who make a positive difference in the world. Congregational leaders need to learn how to GO FISH! in their communities.

Just as we do not expect fish to come and simply jump into a boat because it is there, we cannot expect that somehow people will simply come and jump into our congregations because we are there.

The first handbook, workbook, and DVD of the GO FISH! series encourages congregations to focus on outreach ministries which meet the pressing needs of people in their own communities.

Future emphases for the GO FISH! series will offer effective ways of following up with first-time visitors, how to share faith personally in an authentic and meaningful way, how to reach new persons through children and family ministries, how to use various public media outlets in reaching our communities, and how to develop a climate of hospitality for persons who are not yet a part of a congregation.

Each title of the series is written by a practicing local pastor or lay leader in a congregation that is effectively reaching out and leading people to become followers of Jesus Christ.

Our goal is not simply to enable congregations to grow in participation and membership. Our goal is that congregations will become vital centers of loving service for the spiritual and personal needs of the people of their communities so that the world will be transformed into a compassionate, just, inclusive and Christ-like community.

The ultimate goal of the GO FISH! series is to be used by God for the transformation of the people in our communities from fear to faith, from complacency to compassion, and from greed to generosity. Our hope is that more and more people will become followers of Jesus, who is still at work in transforming and redeeming our world.

—Dr. Kent Millard, Lead Pastor
St. Luke's UMC
Indianapolis, IN

Acknowledgements

We are indebted to many people at St. Luke's United Methodist Church who did the "heavy lifting" in helping our congregation to become a more outward-focused congregation.

We are especially indebted to the leadership team who first led us to a new vision of "being transformed by God so God could use us to transform the world into a compassionate, just, inclusive, and Christ-like community."

Then we are indebted to the Together In Ministry Everyday task force who prayed, reflected, organized and encouraged the whole congregation to become outward focused in all of our ministry areas. They helped us to see that this was not simply one other program of our congregation, but a change of our church culture so we are mindful of the impact and responsibility we have on and towards our local and global community as Christians.

We are also indebted to all the members and friends of our congregation who actually gave more of their T.I.M.E. to serve people in need in our congregation and community and beyond. Literally hundreds of persons are giving more of their time, talent and treasure in loving and serving hundreds of other people in the name of Jesus Christ, and everyone is being blessed in the process. The one comment we have heard over and over again is "I received far more than I gave." Our motivation for caring for others is not so that we will be blessed, but the reality is that when we unselfishly share our lives and love with others we cannot help but be blessed.

But most of all we want to give the glory to God who inspires, prods, challenges, supports, and blesses all those who seek to carry out Jesus command to "tend my sheep."

Kent Millard
Lori Crantford

June 2008

Creating a T.I.M.E. Program

St. Luke's United Methodist Church in Indianapolis, Indiana is a congregation of about 6,000 people on the north side of Indianapolis, Indiana. Weekly worship attendance at St. Luke's and The Garden, our off-site satellite ministry, averages just above three thousand at ten regular worship services.

The mission, vision, and method adopted by St. Luke's can work together at any size church to lay not only the foundation of your faith community but serve as guides by which you measure the work that you do.

Mission: To become an open community of Christians gathering to seek, celebrate, live, and share the love of God for all creation.

Vision: To be transformed by God and transforming the world into a compassionate, just, inclusive, Christ-like community.

Method: To experience God's unconditional love, embrace hope, grow in faith, and become empowered by our passion for ministry and service in the world.

Through a continued process of discernment and discussion, the leadership (lay and clergy) determine that the congregation should concentrate on the concept of outward-focused ministry. Building on internal successes in worship, music, and education programs, the church's leaders determined that parishioners should be encouraged, empowered, and equipped for ministry outside the church's walls. Both laity and clergy will to envision your church less as a destination where "faith" happens, and more as a "spiritual airport" where the faithful come to be strengthened specifically so that they can leave to engage in ministries of service, education, and advocacy.

Like a sculptor revealing his finished product under a lump of clay, these processes reveal a program that would enroll the entire church into being in ministry in real, everyday ways. The idea is based on these key elements:

1. All people, regardless of age, disability, experience, knowledge, or qualification have the capacity to keep learning and growing, and all are called.

2. Ministry is not an extraordinary activity. It is not something you do once a week or for an hour a day. It is a way of being, an identity, a way of understanding who we are—that as disciples of Jesus Christ, everything, every moment, every skill, every resource we have is God's and is meant for ministry. We are God's physical presence in this world. Through us, in every way, every day, through all we say and do and who we are, God is seeking to communicate love. This is ministry.

3. Ministry is outward-focused on the individual level and on the corporate level. It is focused on those immediately around us at home and at work and everywhere in between, and it is focused on those with whom we will never come into contact. Ministry calls us beyond our own lives and our comfort zone. Christ focused on the poor and marginalized and vulnerable. So must we. We cannot be satisfied as a church simply to be more caring amongst ourselves–we must constantly be engaged on behalf of the poor in contexts beyond our walls.

Thus, Together In Ministry Everyday (T.I.M.E.) is born.

With these elements as a foundation, the T.I.M.E. committee of your church can work in two major directions:

1. A church-wide survey should be conducted to discover how outward-focused your congregation already is, and to celebrate what is already being accomplished. You want to find out specific service activities that are

already a part of individual lives. You may also use the Survey tool on page 117 to test for readiness.

2. A T.I.M.E. subcommittee begins work on a theme entitled *90 Minutes in 90 Days*, or *90 in 90* for short. The concept of *90 in 90* is to lift up different themes throughout the year and give individuals the opportunity to test the waters of outreach ministry by giving 90 minutes of service to an organization over a 90-day period of time.

We learned at St. Luke's that we had a very outward-focused church body with many persons already engaged in service activities, and that the congregation would be receptive to this type of church-wide initiative. The first *90 in 90* Connections Expo—a Sunday morning opportunity for not-for-profit organizations and internal church ministries to present theme-based needs and offer chances for individuals to become volunteers in the area of their choosing–was highly successful. Over time, the *90 in 90* initiative has proved successful in creating long-term, outward-focused volunteers.

T.I.M.E. is conceived as an umbrella program that would call the congregation to be in service empowered by God—to discover, embrace, and actively share our gifts and talents in our communities and the world. The *90 Minutes in 90 Days* process invites persons to focus on a particular issue of human struggle and social concern, extending a compelling call to each of us to be involved in opportunities of learning, service, and advocacy.

Over a two or three year period, a congregation might embrace the following *90 in 90* themes:
Poverty and Socio-Economic Justice
Peace and Reconciliation
Education and Literacy
Health, Hunger, and Wholeness
Caring for Creation
Bridging the Generations
Our Health, Our World, Our People
Creating Community
Love, Serve, and Care for One Another . . . Everyday

Each 90-day cycle kicks off with a Connections Expo. Community organizations and existing church ministries that fit with the ministry theme are provided a table to display their materials and offer ministry opportunities to church members. The *90 in 90* team also prepares a printed directory with contact information for each of the organizations represented at the Expo. After the Connections Expo, a Consecration Sunday blesses the efforts of members who have committed to ministries of service, advocacy, and learning on behalf of the ministry theme. Then, at the end of three months, a Celebration Sunday acknowledges the congregation's work in ministry and shares stories of how each member has been in ministry over the last 90 days.

The T.I.M.E. leaders and committee members also work with various groups within the church to create additional program opportunities throughout the 90 days to help members focus on the specific ministry theme, together, for a set period of time. For example, during "Our Health, Our World, Our People," a major emphasis was Sierra Leone. A large mission team was going to Sierra Leone, taking contributions from the congregation to conduct life-changing, life-saving work in a part of the world that has been devastated by civil war.

As part of the "Our Health, Our World, Our People" theme, we launched a "One Church, One Book" initiative, encouraging everyone to read *A Long Way Gone: Memoirs of a Boy Soldier* by Ishmael Beah, who had been a child soldier during the Sierra Leone civil war. Several Sunday school classes and book groups adopted the book and invited all who were interested to come discuss it. Local Sierra Leoneans came to St. Luke's for a cultural exchange. The movie "Blood Diamonds" (about the diamond trade in Sierra Leone and its effects on the country) was shown and discussed. Hundreds and hundreds of pairs of sneakers were collected for months to be sent to Sierra Leone for children who have no shoes. A Hunger Banquet was held where participants were able to experience first-hand how very little food is available to very many people in the world. Our youth held a 30-hour famine, and a church-wide food pantry drive was held.

Those are large-scale examples of the work that can be done by a large congregation. But the work of T.I.M.E. needn't be grand in scope. The word "everyday" is in the name for a reason. Members of the congregation are encouraged to be in ministry everyday, in everyday ways. Here are everyday ways to be in ministry with these topics;

T.I.M.E. in My Car
Pray when you encounter emergency vehicles, accident scenes, roadside vagrants, a surly driver; park farther out to open spaces for those who need them.

T.I.M.E. at Work
Accept criticism with grace; deliver criticism with grace; ask someone new out to lunch; re-read e-mails before you send them.

T.I.M.E. at School
When buying school supplies remember those in need; volunteer your time in a classroom; make room for a new friend on the bus or at lunch.

T.I.M.E. During the Holidays
Give your change to the Salvation Army ringers and thank them for what they are doing; shovel your neighbor's walk; send a greeting to a serviceman or woman overseas; spend silly time with a child; remember the reason for the season.

T.I.M.E. for the New Year
Resolve to invite one new person to come to church this year; resolve to count your blessings more, and your complaints less; resolve to be a better steward of all God has given you.

T.I.M.E. for Our Health
Remember your body's a temple, so treat it like it's the Ritz; join a group that raises funds to cure cancer or other disease; pray without ceasing for those who are suffering.

T.I.M.E. in Our Community
Write a letter of encouragement and congratulations to a new graduate; honor the mothers and fathers in your life in May and June; plant a tree or flowers.

In a church newsletter the pastor might send a message like this:

Time. We spend a lot of time talking about time. "This will only take a second." "When you get a minute." "My, how time flies." "We had the time of our lives." "Where does the time go?" "I don't have time." When a new year begins it is an opportunity to focus our attention on "time" in our lives and how we will invest it.

There are 60 minutes in an hour, 1,440 minutes in a day, 525,600 minutes in a year and 42,048,000 minutes in a lifetime of 80 years. Most of us will have several million minutes to live in this world, so the question is: how will we invest these God-given minutes? Every minute we have is a gift from God, and we get to decide how we will use them. Carl Sandburg said, "Time is the coin of your life. It is the only coin you have, and only you can determine how it will be spent. Be careful lest you let other people spend it for you."

If time is a coin, then how would you like to spend your time?

Before embarking on a T.I.M.E. program of your own, each congregation should ask itself these questions:

1. Is becoming an outward-focused congregation our passion? Is this a part of our church's DNA?

2. If so, spend time in prayer and reflection asking, "Why has God put us in this particular community? How are we responding to our cultural settings? Are we honoring the work that has been set before us?"

3. If time is a coin, then how would your congregation like to spend its time?

Through prayer, discernment, discussion, and too much church coffee, the clergy, lay leadership and staff of St. Luke's asked themselves those questions. When the answer was clearly "yes," the T.I.M.E. sculpture revealed itself. It is still a beautiful work in progress as the living love of God continues to mold and shape the lives of everyone involved—both those reaching out to make a difference, and those who receive much-needed compassion.

How to Use the T.I.M.E. Workbook

You have in your hands a practical guide for getting *Together in Ministry Everyday* (T.I.M.E.) started in your congregation. Whether you have one hundred or ten thousand members, your church can thrive with outward-focused ministry in your community and in the world. In order to implement a T.I.M.E. strategy, you will need to decide if your church will focus on all five ministry areas in the T.I.M.E. Workbook or if you will choose only one or two ministry areas. Pray and discern together what you think God is calling your church to do. When you've done that, gather ministry teams together around the areas you will be working on. Each team member will need his or her own T.I.M.E. Workbook.

Each ministry focus in the T.I.M.E. Workbook has a three-session study. Ministry teams should follow the study outline and then put their plans into action. The studies are meant to delve a little deeper into each theme, provide some biblical insight, and inspire the teams to action. The studies don't necessarily need a leader, but it might be good to have people volunteer to facilitate each session. You'll want someone taking good notes when you begin the planning phase of your work together.

The last session of each study includes a segment from the T.I.M.E. DVD. The DVD clips are inspirational stories of people who are spending time in ministry everyday. The purpose of the DVD is for your group to take a peek into what other folks are doing and how lives are being transformed to see where it might lead your group in ministry.

Your group may also want to have the T.I.M.E. Devotions for your personal devotion time. The Devotions are written by people who have participated in T.I.M.E. and have stories of transformation and hope. They promise even more inspiration to fill your spirit with a passion to serve.

Blessings on your outward-focused journey. May God inspire your congregation to great work as you commit to time in ministry everyday.

There is always the danger that we may just do the work for the sake of the work. This is where the respect and the love and the devotion come in—that we do it to God, to Christ, and that's why we try to do it as beautifully as possible.

— Mother Teresa

That's What It's All About

What if the hokey pokey is all it really is about?

That's the question singer/songwriter Jimmy Buffett lays out for us. On the face of it, the question seems absurd. Of course the hokey pokey isn't what "it's" all about! Life is about so much more than a silly phrase—a cheesy party song. If that's true, can "*The Chicken Dance*" as our national anthem be far behind?

But hold on. Turns out there may be something to this question. Dr. Karen Oliveto, pastor of Glide Memorial United Methodist Church, discussed this concept as she addressed the congregation. She shared a fascinating, possible origin of the phrase "hokey pokey."

If you look on Wikipedia for the story of the "hokey pokey," you find that it has roots in the Christian church—sort of. Hokey pokey has also been known as hokey cokey and is derived from "hocus pocus," of the magical lexicon. Hocus pocus is a distortion of *hoc enim est corpus meum*, or "this is my body," the words of consecration for Eucharist. In traditional Catholic practice, this phrase is used at the point of transubstantiation—when the elements become flesh and blood. Puritans mocked this idea and likened the phrase and the act itself to "magic." One Anglican provost suggests that the hokey pokey dance mimics the Latin mass as well. The priest turns his back to the congregation and the people can't hear him or see his movements. The legend is that all that the congregants could hear as the priest "turned himself about" was "hokey pokey."

However, Dr. Oliveto gives new meaning to the hokey pokey. She suggests that in being true, accepting Christians, committed to live as reflections of God's unconditional love, that we should do as the hokey pokey says: Put our whole selves in! When we put our whole selves into ministry, into loving ourselves and others as God loves us, then we are transformed and equipped to go shakin' God's love all about! So maybe, just maybe, when we do the hokey pokey and we turn ourselves around, that really is *what it's all about.*

Putting our whole selves in is the concept behind being *Together in Ministry Everyday* (T.I.M.E.). This workbook is designed to partner with the concepts discussed in the T.I.M.E. handbook to help you put the concept of outreach, or *ex-vangelism*, to work on personal, congregational, and community levels. The DVD offers further inspiration with personal stories of how churches reaching out into the community truly have an impact, one person at a time.

Each chapter gives examples and questions to help you dig deep within yourself. Let the questions and stories inspire you to discover how you can follow Jesus' mandate to "go and do likewise"—to reach out and care for people in need who are likely right in your own community.

While you may find yourself getting excited about the concepts presented, chomping at the bit to get out there and make a difference, just remember: you don't have to do everything. You don't have to feed and teach and heal and hug and shelter. Ministry burnout isn't pretty. Trust me on that one. Pick the areas that appeal to you the most, the one or maybe two that really tug at your heartstrings. Or pick the ones that make the most sense for the connections that already exist within your church, your community, or with colleagues, friends, or family members. Is there a struggling food pantry in your area that could really benefit from a support system? Great! Take that one on, and let someone else hug a tree or save a whale.

It doesn't take a mission trip across time zones or a bank account the size of Bill Gates's to make a significant difference in the lives of others. Everyday people doing ordinary things with extraordinary love have already shown us the way. Even as he struggled with a lifelong terminal disease, teenage visionary Mattie Stepanek believed he had a voice for peace that should be heard. Mattie put his whole self into his vision and mission and, hampered as his whole self was by a disease that tragically ended his life at the age of 14, he did not let that deter him from his course. Mattie viewed the world and all people as a "mosaic of gifts." What a beautiful, inspiring concept—each of us with God-given gifts that are unique on their own, yet when placed with the unique gifts of others create a thing of grace and beauty.

When we work *Together in Ministry Everyday*, we put our unique gifts to work in ways that fill us with wonder at what is possible when we put our whole selves in. When others witness the possibilities, they will begin to see God's transforming work in action.

And that's what it's all about.

Chapter One
Feed My Sheep

"Jesus said to him, 'Feed my sheep.'"
—John 21:17

"Where's the beef?"
—Wendy's TV commercial

Session One: **Sharing the Feast**
Session Two: **Together in Ministry Everyday**
Session Three: **Putting Plans into Action**

Session One:
Sharing the Feast

Notes

Opening

Gather as a community and open with prayer. Choose a volunteer to lead a prayer or pray together the following corporate prayer:

"Compassionate God, we are here to put our whole selves into feeding your sheep. Too many of your beloved children go hungry and we want to do something about it. Ignite in us a passion to feed the hungry in our community and around our world. Equip us to do this work. In the name of Christ we pray, amen."

Devotion

Take turns reading aloud the essay "*Not Gonna Get the Feast*."

"Good morning everybody. I sorta just got up so I'm a little tired, but I felt like I had to say this. Something that I've learned from this is how dependent we are on God. I think we forget that cause we just go through our everyday lives and we think that it's us who's getting the food and nurturing ourselves but I think that we have to remember that it's God who keeps providing for us and I think we need to remember how dependent we are on him instead of thinking we are dependent on ourselves."

Notes

"One of the things that I've gotten out of this is knowing that tomorrow— we're like very hungry right now—and knowing that tomorrow we are gonna have, like, a feast, and I know that there are millions of kids that are, like, not gonna get the feast . . . there's millions of kids who are going through the exact same thing we're going through and are gonna wake up tomorrow morning, and they're not gonna get the feast, they're not gonna get anything, it's going to be, like, the same."

These quotations are from teenagers taking a reflective moment during a 30-Hour Famine experience that is designed to raise awareness of hunger issues in the world. After breakfast at church on a Friday morning, their fast began at 8 a.m. The youth answered questions at school and witnessed to friends about hunger as they skipped lunch and fasted through the day. Many of their peers were curious and supportive, while others ridiculed and waved junk food in their faces. After school the youth gathered at the church to share stories, drink juice, and try to get their minds off of their hunger. The youth learned that every hour over 1,200 people die of hunger or hunger-related illness in the world. They made 1,200 crosses out of Popsicle sticks to display on the front lawn of the church, a task that they found took much more than one hour. They worshipped together. They worked with a budget of $1,100 a month (a figure derived from determining the low-end costs of basic life necessities in the Indianapolis area) and the Internet to see how they could live on that amount of money in a large, urban setting and what they were willing to sacrifice. And, they slept as long as possible into the day on Saturday. After 30 hours the group broke the fast with a feast and reflected on faith and hunger and how to share the experience with others.

Have you ever been hungry? *Really* hungry? There's stomach-growling hungry, which is mildly uncomfortable. And then there's sugar-low hungry, where you start to feel

Notes

lightheaded and weak. But how hard was it for you to remedy? How long did you have to wait until you could eat? Fifteen minutes? Thirty? Maybe an hour or two?

Guess what most of us say in these situations: "I'm starving!"

The truth is, most of us know little about hunger and have probably never experienced starvation. Relief is usually just a reach into the pantry or a fast-food stop away. For anyone who has ever traveled to an underdeveloped nation, the lack of instant food gratification smacks you right in the face. This may be hard to believe, but you will not find Starbucks, Subway, or McDonald's on the rutted road between Nairobi and Eldoret, Kenya. Not even a Cracker Barrel! If you get hungry, you'll have to eat and drink what you brought with you. If you didn't bring anything with you, you'll need to make friends fast with the forward-thinking traveling companion who brought the chocolate chunk granola bars and bottled water.

Instant food gratification is an unknown concept to millions of truly starving individuals around the world. As you sit and read this, it is likely that you are with a group of others who gathered together with a common goal of becoming more outward-focused, to breathe life into Jesus' mandate "go and do likewise." And since you're probably doing this in a church, there's even a better chance that food is involved. Did you walk into a room with muffins and bagels? Pizza and salad? Sandwiches and chips? Mouth-watering cookies and coffee?

It's OK if you did. You don't have to feel bad (unless you're cheating on your diet, and that's between you, God, and your scale). But take a moment to realize the stark difference between your reality and the reality of so many of our fellow men, women, and children. For them, food is simply not within their reach.

Notes

The thing about hunger is that, while tragic enough on its own, it becomes a vicious, no-holds-barred partner with disease. Nutrition is a vital component in the battle against HIV/AIDS and many other life-threatening illnesses. Without proper nutrition, disease-ravaged bodies cannot possibly fight off infection. For these people, being hungry isn't about being moderately uncomfortable. It's about staying alive.

Even in our own country, starvation levels are staggering. America's Second Harvest—The Nation's Food Bank Network is the United States' largest charitable hunger-relief organization. The network of more than two hundred member food banks and food-rescue organizations, serves all 50 states, the District of Columbia, and Puerto Rico. The America's Second Harvest Network secures and distributes more than two billion pounds of donated food and grocery products annually.

Each year, the America's Second Harvest Network provides food assistance to more than 25 million low-income, hungry people in the United States, including more than nine million children and nearly three million seniors.

The following statistics from the year 2006 are from Second Harvest's website. For more info, log on to www.secondharvest.org. You can find state-by-state statistics, food bank locators and much more.

Poverty:

- Nearly 37 million people (12.3%) were in poverty.
- 7.6 (9.8%) million families were in poverty.
- 20.2 million (10.8%) people aged 18-64 were in poverty.
- 2.8 million (17.4%) children under the age of 18 were in poverty.
- 3.4 million (9.4%) seniors 65 and older were in poverty.

Notes

Food Insecurity (Low Food Security and Very Low Security) and Food Insecurity With Hunger (Very Low Security)

- 35.5 million Americans lived in food-insecure households, 22.8 million adults and 12.6 million children.
- Households with children reported food insecurity at almost double the rate for those without children, 15.6% compared to 8.5%.
- Households with seniors (1.59 million households) were food-insecure (low food security and very low food security).

Child Hunger Facts:

According to Second Harvest, "the problem of childhood hunger is not simply a moral issue. Scientific evidence suggests that hungry children are less likely to become productive citizens. A child who is unequipped to learn because of hunger and poverty is more likely to be poor as an adult. As such, the existence of childhood hunger in the United States threatens future American prosperity."

Current Statistics:

- Over nine million children are estimated to be served by the America's Second Harvest Network, over two million of whom are ages five and under, representing nearly 13% of all children under age 18 in the United States and over 72% of all children in poverty.
- Proper nutrition is vital to the growth and development of children, particularly low-income children. Sixty-two percent of all client households with children under the age of 18 participated in a school lunch program, but only 13% participated in a summer feeding program that provides free food when school is out.
- Fifty-one percent of client households with children under the age of three participated in the Special Supplemental Nutrition Program for Women, Infants, and Children (WIC).

Notes

- Nearly 41% of emergency food providers in the America's Second Harvest Network reported "many more children in the summer" being served by their programs.
- Research indicates that even mild undernutrition experienced by young children during critical periods of growth impacts their behavior, their school performance, and their overall cognitive development.
- In fiscal year 2005, 50% of children were food stamp recipients.
- During the 2005 federal fiscal year, 17.5 million low-income children received free or reduced-price meals through the National School Lunch Program. Unfortunately, just under two million of these same income-eligible children participated in the Summer Food Service Program that same year (www.secondharvest.org).

As you can see, people are suffering in our own schools, neighborhoods, and nearby communities. *"There are children who are, like, not gonna get the feast."* Even though we all may be dependent on God and not on ourselves, that doesn't mean that God is going to bring us all take-out. God has given us the tools to do God's work in this world. This work is about feeding hungry people. It's not just about lunch. It's about the feeding of spirit as well, about love, and nourishment. Talk about an extra-value meal!

Storytelling

Take a few minutes to share personal stories of hunger. You may also want to share any insights you gained from the Feed My Sheep chapter in the T.I.M.E. Handbook. Here are some questions to guide your discussion:

- *In what ways have you experienced or witnessed the hungry being fed?*
- *Why do you think you are feeling led to participate in hunger ministries?*

- *What is your dream for the hunger ministry in your church?*

Notes

Bible Study

Divide into small groups to read the following Scriptures and discuss the questions.

Read: Matthew 7:9-10; 12:3-4; 14:16

Discuss: What level of importance do you think Jesus places on feeding the hungry?
What do you find most challenging in these verses?

____
____
____
____

Read: Matthew 25:35-40

Discuss: Imagine yourself in that conversation with Jesus. What is going through your mind?
How often do you see the face of Christ when you see a homeless person?
What do you find most challenging in this passage?

____
____
____
____

Read: Luke16:19-31

Discuss: What are some modern-day parallels to these Bible characters?
What is Jesus saying to us about hunger in this passage?
What do you find most challenging in this Scripture lesson?

Notes

Read: John 21:1-14

Discuss: What does this passage tell you about the importance of a meal?

Why would you study this Scripture passage when thinking about feeding the hungry?

Jesus showed love to his disciples by offering breakfast after a long night of fishing. How can you show love to hungry people in times that might feel like a "long night?"

When the small groups are finished, gather again as a large group and share insights.

Closing

As you end your ministry team meeting, gather in a circle for prayers of the people. Select someone to begin the prayer and someone to close the prayer. During the prayer, each person should lift up a prayer for the work of your ministry team. Respond to each prayer by saying together, "Lord, in your mercy, hear our prayer."

Homework and Business

If you haven't already, you may want to select a leader to facilitate your group meetings. It may also be helpful to have a secretary who can help the group stay informed about projects you'll take on.

For your next meeting, you'll want to read through Session Two: Together in Ministry Everyday. Be prepared to discuss your homework. Don't worry though—you won't be graded on your performance!

Notes

Session Two:
Together in Ministry Everyday

Notes

Opening

Gather as a community and open with prayer. Choose a volunteer to lead a prayer or pray together the following corporate prayer:

"Compassionate God, we are here to put our whole selves into feeding your sheep. Too many of your beloved children go hungry, and we want to do something about it. Ignite in us a passion to feed the hungry in our community and around our world. Equip us to do this work. In the name of Christ we pray, amen."

Storytelling

Discuss where you've sensed fullness and where you've sensed hunger since your last group meeting. If you need to, use the following questions to prompt discussion:

- *How have you seen God at work lately?*
- *In what ways have you personally experienced fullness?*
- *In what ways have you experienced hunger?*
- *What do you know about hunger that you didn't know last week?*

T.I.M.E.

Before your meeting, work through these questions and be

Notes

prepared to discuss your answers. For your group meeting, depending on the size of your group, you may want to divide into smaller groups to talk about your answers to these questions.

T

Take a look around.

- Take off your blinders and ask yourself: am I ignoring local or world hunger issues?

- What is your congregation doing in the area of hunger? What improvements could be made?

- What connections exist within your congregation? Do you have any connections to local or world hunger ministries?

I

Identify and investigate.

- Where is there need?

Notes

- Who are the contacts with whom our group should connect?
- What do these contacts need from us in order for our group to connect with their mission?

Meditate and motivate.

M

- How is God speaking to me about hunger?

- What does my heart tell me?

- How can I make a difference?

Embrace and encourage.

E

- I'm ready to roll up my sleeves and get started. Mother Teresa said, *"There are no great things, only small things with great love."* Name three small things you can do with great love in the area of hunger.

Notes

- *How are you living out your faith through this work? What kind of impact is your faith work having on you? On others around you?*

___

___

___

___

- *How does this work reflect on the mission and vision of your church?*

___

___

___

___

If you divided into smaller groups, gather the large group together and share any highlights from your conversations.

Closing

As you end your ministry team meeting, gather in a circle for prayers of the people. Select someone to begin the prayer and someone to close the prayer. During the prayer, each person should lift up a prayer for the work of your ministry team. Respond to each prayer by saying together, "Lord, in your mercy, hear our prayer."

Homework/Business

Session three is a planning meeting. Determine how to begin your work and what the needs and various roles might be. Assign tasks and research that will be discussed at your next ministry team meeting. Plan to create a plan for action at your next meeting.

Session Three:
Putting Plans into Action

Notes

Opening

Gather as a community and open with prayer. Choose a volunteer to lead a prayer or pray together the following corporate prayer:

"Compassionate God, we are here to put our whole selves in to feeding your sheep. Too many of your beloved children go hungry, and we want to do something about it. Ignite in us a passion to feed the hungry in our community and around our world. Equip us to do this work. In the name of Christ we pray, amen."

Storytelling

Discuss where you've seen moments of fullness or hunger since your last group meeting. If you need to, use the following questions to prompt discussion:

- *How have you seen God at work lately?*
- *In what ways have you personally experienced God's fullness through the love and compassion of another person?*
- *Where do you see hunger and fullness in the world?*

Inspiration

View the DVD segment, "Feed My Sheep." Then, discuss the following questions.

Notes

- *What spoke the loudest to you in the video?*

- *Did anything make your heart leap?*

- *How can your group join in local and global hunger ministries to feed God's sheep?*

Planning

What are your plans for a hunger ministry?

How would describe your work to others in your congregation in order to invite them to join you?

Notes

What needs to be done and who will do the work?

____
____
____
____

Closing

As you end your ministry team meeting, gather in a circle for prayers of the people. Select someone to begin the prayer and someone to close the prayer. During the prayer, each person should lift up a prayer for healing or for the work of your ministry team. Respond to each prayer by saying together, "Lord, in your mercy, hear our prayer."

Benediction

Read aloud the benediction and then "go and do likewise."

"May the God of all fullness fill our hearts and minds with courage, conviction, compassion, and love as we seek to feed God's lambs in this world. May we feel the power of the Holy Spirit in our actions and share the love of Christ with everyone we meet. Amen."

Chapter Two
Teach My Sheep

"Then Jesus began to speak and taught them saying . . ."
—Matthew 5:2

"If you promise not to believe everything your child says happens at school, I'll promise not to believe everything he says happens at home."
—Anonymous teacher

"A hundred years from now, it will not matter what my bank account was, the sort of house I lived in, or the kind of car I drove . . . but the world may be different because I was important in the life of a child."
—Forest E. Witcraft

Session 1: **Being Important in the Life of a Child**
Session 2: **Time in Ministry Everyday**
Session 3: **Putting Plans into Action**

Session One:
Being Important in the Life of a Child

Opening

Notes

Gather as a community and open with prayer. Choose a volunteer to lead a prayer or pray together the following corporate prayer:

"Teacher God, thank you for the ways you show us what it means to be a follower of Jesus Christ. You lead us and teach us through your word and through our relationships. Give us vision and courage to teach your sheep. Show us a path to a teaching ministry and fill us with love and wisdom to do the work. Through Christ our Lord, we pray, amen."

Devotion

Take turns reading aloud the essay "*Reading, 'Rithmetic, and Pineapple Tidbits.*"

Reading, 'Rithmetic, and Pineapple Tidbits

In 1993 a novice teacher named Erin Gruwell stepped into her first classroom at Wilson High School in Long Beach, California. She came dressed in pearls to her inner-city post, and was met by students who had been written off by the educational system. They were divided by race and completely intractable; they were members of gangs, each with firsthand experience of violence, guns, drugs, and juvenile detention. They appeared to care about no one or nothing but themselves and the friends inside their racial circles.

Notes

This novice teacher would not be deterred by these seemingly insurmountable odds. Despite the initial lack of respect in the classroom, which carried through to the teacher's lounge, where her methods met with scorn and her caring attitude was widely discouraged, Gruwell transformed her students' lives. On the website freedomwritersfoundation.org, the students of Room 203 at Wilson High that year tell their story:

"Following the Rodney King riots and the O.J. Simpson trial, the mood in our city was unsettling, and on our first day of high school, we had only three things in common: we hated school, we hated our teacher, and we hated each other.

"Whether it was official or not, we all knew that we had been written off. Low test scores, juvenile hall, alienation, and racial hostility helped us fit the labels the educational system placed on us: 'unteachable,' 'below average,' and 'delinquents.' Somehow, Ms. G recognized our similarities, and used them to unite us. She gave us books written by teenagers that we could relate to, and it was through these books that we began to realize that if we could relate to a little girl who lived on the other side the world, fifty years before we did, we could certainly relate to each other.

"We felt like Anne Frank, trapped in a cage, and identified with the violence in Zlata Filipovic's life [a girl who lived through war-torn Sarajevo]. We were so inspired by the stories of Anne and Zlata, that we wrote letters to Miep Gies [a Dutch citizen who hid Anne Frank and her family, and who discovered and preserved Anne's diary], and to Zlata, in hopes that they would come to Long Beach and share their stories with us. When Miep visited us, she challenged us to keep Anne's memory alive and "passed the baton" to us. It was then that we decided to begin chronicling our lives.

Notes

"We began writing anonymous journal entries about the adversities that we faced in our everyday lives. We wrote about gangs, immigration, drugs, violence, abuse, death, anorexia, dyslexia, teenage love, weight issues, divorce, suicide, and all the other issues we never had the chance to express before. We discovered that writing is a powerful form of self expression that could help us deal with our past and move forward. Room 203 was like Anne's attic or Zlata's basement, it was our safe haven, where we could cry, laugh, and share our stories without being judged" (www.freedomwritersfoundation.org...About_Freedom_Writers.htm).

Eventually, the students' writings were compiled into a book called *The Freedom Writers Diary*, which several years later was made into a movie called "The Freedom Writers." The students decided to call themselves the Freedom Writers after they learned about the Freedom Riders who fought against segregation during the Civil Rights Movement.

According to freedomwritersfoundation.org, "The impact of the Freedom Writers' story has been felt far beyond Room 203 in Long Beach. The book is now taught in classrooms across the country, Erin Gruwell and the Freedom Writers speak at various schools, juvenile detention centers, and conferences around the globe, and the foundation has even begun training teachers to replicate and evolve Erin Gruwell's teaching methods."

Not all of us can teach in a classroom like Erin Gruwell. But we can follow her example of transforming the lives of young people, of being one caring person who will exemplify God's love through our commitment to caring about the education of our youth.

The phrase "I'll teach you a lesson you'll never forget" often carries a negative connotation. But what if you took that

Notes

phrase and turned it to the positive? What if you were able to teach a child a lesson he will never forget? A lesson of one hour spent delving into the treasures of a book with children who struggle with reading? A lesson of making a field trip possible for a student who would not otherwise be able to go? A lesson of having a child know, just by your presence in the classroom, that you value her education?

My personal experience is that there is nothing so rewarding as spending time volunteering in a school. I was fortunate to be able to spend great amounts of time in the public elementary school my two sons attended. They are a year apart in age, so my time there was condensed and intense. The relationships I formed with the majority of those teachers are relationships I cherish and some of which I still maintain. The respect I gained for them was and remains immense. Donald D. Quinn says it all: "If a doctor, lawyer, or dentist had 40 people in his office at one time, all of whom had different needs, and some of whom didn't want to be there and were causing trouble, and the doctor, lawyer, or dentist, without assistance, had to treat them all with professional excellence for nine months, then he might have some conception of the classroom teacher's job."

During my time in the school, I helped children sort colors and shapes, worked with them as they developed reading skills, and was a tearful witness at the Marriage of Q & U (replete with Q as bride, U as groom, other alphabet wedding party members and a very solemn ceremony followed by a lively reception). I helped children learn to skip (and I got to skip too!), dressed as the school mascot many times, and watched with trepidation and awe as each child dropped a self-made Egg Protector first from the curb, then from a chair, and finally from a ladder. Would the egg break? What potential victory or tragedy lies beneath the duct tape and cardboard and foam? Oh, the agony!

Notes

I have wrapped my arms tightly around a child who was frightened standing on a bridge over a cavern in a cave on a field trip ("Mrs. Crantford saved my life!" she later told her teacher), and taken another suddenly green-faced child to the restroom in the nick of time. And I wouldn't have missed for the world the time I was simply present in the classroom to hear during a contextual reading lesson, "I get really excited when my mom packs p__________ in my lunch." In a classroom of second graders, you'd expect "pizza!" or "potato chips!" or "pudding!" But a hand quickly zoomed into the air, and as the teacher called on the student, he shouted out with great enthusiasm: "pineapple tidbits!"

There is no end to the rewards that result from involving yourself in education. Obviously, I have been the recipient of those rewards, which was not my intent but an unexpected, wonderful gift. To this day, as my children approach high school, there are students who still holler out "Hi, Mrs. Crantford!" to me across the hallway, children I no longer recognize as they have aged, but they remember me. (Which clearly means I have not aged at all.)

We don't have to be an Erin Gruwell, or an Annie Sullivan, the legally blind teacher of Helen Keller, or our recent most inspiring teacher, Professor Randy Pausch, who taught the world how to live in the face of death. We only have to follow Jesus' perfect example of teaching by example—showing them God's love.

Teaching the world's "sheep" needn't be limited to the classroom. Coach a team. Share woodworking skills. Start a child's knitting group, yoga class, cooking club, photography workshop. The sky is the limit (unless you are an astronomy expert, in which case the sky is just the entry point!). The examples of Jesus teaching are endless. Ours are only beginning. Where will you start?

Notes

Storytelling

Take a few minutes to share memories from your experience in schools. You may also want to share any insights from the Teach My Sheep chapter in the T.I.M.E. Handbook. Here are some questions to guide your discussion:

- *What was your experience in school? Support? Apathy? Opportunity? Defeat?*
- *Why do you think God is calling you to be part of a teaching ministry?*
- *What is your dream for the teaching ministry in your church?*

Bible Study

Divide into small groups to read the following Scriptures and discuss the questions.

Read: Matthew 5:1-26

Discuss: Describe Jesus' teaching style found in this chapter.
What can we learn about teaching from Jesus' sermon?
What are some major themes of these lessons from Jesus?

____

____

____

Read: Matthew 18:1-5

Discuss: What does it mean to "become like a child"?
Why are children so important to Jesus?
What are the implications for a teaching ministry in our church?

____

____

____

Notes

Read: Matthew 28:16-20

Discuss: What does Jesus tell the disciples to do?
Why would teaching be part of the commission?
What are the implications for a teaching ministry in our church?

___

___

___

Closing

As you end your ministry team meeting, gather in a circle for prayers of the people. Select someone to begin the prayer and someone to close the prayer. During the prayer, each person should lift up a prayer for the work of your ministry team. Respond to each prayer by saying together, "Lord, in your mercy, hear our prayer."

Homework and Business

If you haven't already, you may want to select a leader to facilitate your group meetings. It may also be helpful to have a secretary who can help the group stay informed about projects you'll take on. For your next meeting, you'll want to read through Session Two: Together in Ministry Everyday. Be prepared to discuss your homework. Don't worry though—you won't be graded on your performance!

Session Two: **Together in Ministry Everyday**

Prepare for your next group meeting by working through the T.I.M.E. outline. Pray through the questions and make notes that you can share with the group.

Notes

Opening

Gather as a community and open with prayer. Choose a volunteer to lead a prayer or pray together the following corporate prayer:

"Teacher God, thank you for the ways you show us what it means to be a follower of Jesus Christ. You lead us and teach us through your word and through our relationships. Give us vision and courage to teach your sheep. Show us a path to a teaching ministry and fill us with love and wisdom to do the work. Through Christ our Lord, we pray, amen."

Storytelling

Discuss any moment in which you've learned something new or gained new insight since your last group meeting. If you need to, use the following questions to prompt discussion:

- *How did you experience God through a teaching moment this week?*
- *How have you seen God at work through education lately?*
- *In what ways have you personally experienced God's love through a teacher or mentor?*

Notes

T.I.M.E.

Before your meeting, work through these questions and be prepared to discuss your answers. For your group meeting, depending on the size of your group, you may want to divide into smaller groups to talk about your answers to these questions.

T

Take a look around.

- Take off your blinders and ask yourself: Am I ignoring educational needs in our community?

- What is your congregation doing in the area of teaching? What improvements could be made?

- What connections to educational ministries exist within your congregation?

I

Identify and investigate.

- Where is there need for teaching and educational outreach?

Notes

- Who are the contacts with whom our group should connect?
- What do these contacts need from us in order for our group to connect with their mission?

Meditate and motivate.

M

- How is God speaking to me about my role in an educational outreach ministry?

- What does my heart tell me?

- How can I make a difference?

Embrace and encourage.

E

- I'm ready to roll up my sleeves and get started. Mother *Teresa said, "There are no great things, only small things with great love."* Name three small things you can do with great love in the area of education.

Notes

- How are you living out your faith through this work? What kind of impact is your faith work having on you? On others around you?

___

___

___

___

- How might your work on an educational outreach ministry reflect the mission and vision of your church?

___

___

___

___

If you divided into smaller groups, gather the large group together and share any highlights from your conversations.

Closing

As you end your ministry team meeting, gather in a circle for prayers of the people. Select someone to begin the prayer and someone to close the prayer. During the prayer, each person should lift up a prayer for the work of your ministry team. Respond to each prayer by saying together, "Lord, in your mercy, hear our prayer."

Homework/Business

Session three is a planning meeting. Determine how to begin your work and what the needs and various roles might be. Assign tasks and research that will be discussed at your next ministry team meeting. Plan to create a plan for action at your next meeting.

Session Three:

Putting Plans into Action

Notes

Opening

Gather as a community and open with prayer. Choose a volunteer to lead a prayer or pray together the following corporate prayer:

"Teacher God, thank you for the ways you show us what it means to be a follower of Jesus Christ. You lead us and teach us through your word and through our relationships. Give us vision and courage to teach your sheep. Show us a path to a teaching ministry and fill us with love and wisdom to do the work. Through Christ our Lord, we pray, amen."

Storytelling

Discuss where you've seen moments of teaching since your last group meeting. If you need to, use the following questions to prompt discussion:

- *How have you seen God at work through education lately?*
- *In what ways have you personally experienced God's love through the love and kindness of another person?*

Inspiration

View the DVD segment, "Teach My Sheep." Then, discuss the following questions:

Notes

- What spoke the loudest to you in the video?

- Did anything make your heart leap?

- How can your group share God's love through a teaching ministry?

Planning

What are your plans for a teaching ministry?

How would you describe your work to others in your congregation in order to invite them to join you?

What needs to be done and who will do the work?

Notes

____

____

____

____

Closing

As you end your ministry team meeting, gather in a circle for prayers of the people. Select someone to begin the prayer and someone to close the prayer. During the prayer, each person should lift up a prayer for the work of your ministry team. Respond to each prayer by saying together, "Lord, in your mercy, hear our prayer."

Benediction

Read aloud the benediction and then "go and do likewise."

"May the God who teaches us what love is all about fill us with that love and grant us courage to go out and share it. May we find the wisdom, kindness, and gentleness to teach and be taught in our community—to reach outside the walls of our church to bring nurture and care through education. Through Christ our Lord, we pray, amen."

Chapter Three
Heal My Sheep

"Our sorrows and wounds are healed only when we touch them with compassion."

— Buddha

"The only work that will ultimately bring any good to any of us is the work of contributing to the healing of the world."

— Marianne Williamson

Session One: **Healing Is on the Way**
Session Two: **Together in Ministry Everyday**
Session Three: **Putting Plans into Action**

Session One:
Healing Is on the Way

Notes

Opening

Gather as a community and open with prayer. Choose a volunteer to lead a prayer or pray together the following corporate prayer:

"Healing God, we are here to put our whole selves into healing your sheep. Ignite a passion in us to bring healing and compassion to our community and to our world. Equip us to do your healing work. In the name of Christ we pray, amen."

Devotion

Take turns reading aloud the essay "*Boo-Boos, Band-Aids®, and Medical Brigades.*"

Boo-boos, Band-Aids®, and Medical Brigades

"Mommy! Oh, ouch! I have an owie! I fell down and gots a boo-boo! It hurts baaaad!"

Ah, boo-boos. At some point we have all been that child, and many of us have been that mom or dad, aunt or uncle, teacher, friend, or neighbor of a child with a boo-boo. The scraped knee or elbow hurt with the seeming sting factor of a hundred bees and for at least half of those victims, gravel was involved. Probably dirt as well. And heaven help us, blood. In other words: a Greek tragedy in the making.

Notes

Enter the compassionate caring healer. Armed with soap, water, washcloth, antibiotic ointment, a Band-Aid®, and most importantly, a kiss, soon everything was all better.

While the cleansing agents took care of potential germs, they weren't the medicine that sent the child skipping back outside to face the potential dangers of the universe (or the driveway). It was the magic Band-Aid® and kiss that finally caused the heaving sobs to turn to quivering lips and then a bright sweet smile to appear on a salty, tear-stained face. It was love that healed.

Love is why we have Band-Aids®. The concept that "just putting a Band-Aid®" on a problem is a temporary and short-sighted fix is an unfortunate one. The Band-Aid® was the idea of one Earle Dickson, and he didn't mean it as an easy, short-term solution to a bad situation. Earle loved his wife and he just wanted dinner.

See, Earle's wife, Josephine, had knife issues. She was constantly nicking her fingers while she worked in the kitchen. This was 1920 when the only way to protect a cut was to use squares of gauze and tape. These were, of course, cumbersome and required two people to affix. So Earle came up with the idea of putting a small piece of sterile gauze in the center of strips of surgical tape. He would unroll the tape, lay folded gauze over it, then put crinoline on top to keep the tape from sticking to itself, and then he re-rolled the tape. That way, when Josephine got a boo-boo, she could unwind the needed amount of bandage, cut off, and apply what she needed. And get back to making Earle's dinner.

The execs at Johnson & Johnson, where Earle worked, thought this was pretty nifty, so they took his idea and began manufacturing Band-Aids®. These new-fangled bandages didn't take off right away, until a few years later when Johnson &

Notes

Johnson gave them away to Boy Scout troops—a big bunch of boo-boos waiting to happen if ever there was one. The rest is history.

No matter how old we are, we all still get-boo boos in life. Some are relatively minor, the playground variety. Some are major league. Some are made bearable with a hug and a kiss. Some require more serious procedures. Some are curable. And some are not.

While there is no denying the power of the soap/water/wash-cloth and medicine aspect of healing, real healing is so much more than a prescription pad and an IV drip. Healing does not necessarily require a medical degree. Healing is achieved in many amazing and miraculous ways as we reach out in love, compassion, and faith.

Of course, medicine plays a first-round-draft-choice role in healing. Without important advances in medicine, the current inhabitants of planet Earth might be plants and water—none of whom have the slightest need for a computer or a cell phone. Talk about your tragedies!

Medical missions to underdeveloped countries are as important to the soul as they are to the body. People who have lived in virtually hopeless situations are suddenly handed the gift of hope. Without fail, those who went to help return home in awe of how blessed they feel and how much love was shared with them by those they intended to serve. In some ways, it's hard to know whom God blessed the most.

During the ninth annual Medical Brigade in Honduras, a collaborative effort of Vida Nueva United Methodist Church (UMC) in downtown Indianapolis, Metro Ministries for the Indianapolis East and West districts of the South Conference, and St. Luke's UMC, Dr. Bill Whitson was delivering

Notes

medical care to people in mountain villages who have no access to such care. A little girl was being examined by one of the doctors present. He discovered that one eye was not moving properly and sent her to "Dr. Bill," an eye surgeon. Bill discovered there was a sliver of metal in her eye. He borrowed a tool from the trip's oral surgeon and removed the object from the child's eye. While packing up to close the clinic, Bill said, "Now I know why I came. I've just saved a child's eyesight."

The 2008 Medical Brigade consisted of a 21-member team that traveled to Honduras and set up clinics in six different mountain villages. In eight days they treated 2,514 patients. Two of the sites required a three-hour bus ride and when the bus broke down one day, it was a five-hour trip. Five people trained in nursing served as triage, sending people on to one of five doctors as needed. Dr. Dick Lautzenheiser, rheumatologist, drained fluid from joints, relieving painful pressures. He has been there before and was sometimes greeted with smiles from returning patients. Dr. Ron Nellen pulled about three hundred teeth. Dr. Ed Blackburn, general practitioner, and R.B. Mernitz, general surgeon, saw patients with all kinds of illnesses; they prescribed medicines and treatments. Dr. Whitson took with him and distributed almost six hundred pairs of glasses, giving people an opportunity to read and see better. Dr. Beth Kline organized the pharmacy and directed the use of the medicines.

Friendships and goodwill are built in countries where repeated missions take place. Nine years ago Dr. Whitson went to Honduras to take a break from his eye-surgery routine. While working on top of a chicken coop he met a Honduran man who obviously had an eye problem. Dr. Whitson could not resist asking if the man would let him examine him. Subsequently he brought the man, Osman, to the states and performed surgery. Osman and Bill's faces lit

Notes

up when they met again on this trip. Osman is now a part of the ICES Church that hosts the visit. He preached the Sunday the Brigade was there. He and his wife, Suyapa, also a minister, took the team to see the church they are building in their mountain village.

The non-medical members of the team serve an integral healing role as well, cleaning out ears, organizing the waiting crowd of patients, distributing medicines as authorized, working in the pharmacy and helping to set up and dismantle the clinics. They work with the doctors to unpack the much-needed medical supplies shipped over in advance—many of these items donated by church members who, through their donations, become long-distance healers. Pain relievers, vitamins, cough drops, just about any kind of OTC medication imaginable is unavailable to millions of men, women, and children in need.

Prayers are packed alongside those medicines. Prayers of healing, prayers of compassion, prayers of love. And, oh yeah—lots and lots of Band-Aids®, too.

The world has many boo-boos. How can you help the hurt go away?

Storytelling

Take a few minutes to share personal stories of healing. You may also want to share any insights you gained from the Heal My Sheep chapter in the T.I.M.E. Handbook. Here are some questions to guide your discussion:

- *In what ways have you experienced or witnessed healing in your life?*
- *Why do you think you are feeling led to participate in healing ministries?*

Notes

- *What is your dream for the healing ministry in your church?*

Bible Study

Divide into small groups to read the following Scriptures and discuss the questions.

Read: Matthew 8:1-17, 10:5-8, 25:31-46

Discuss: *What are some common elements to these passages about healing?*
Why do you think healing was so important to Jesus?
When it comes to healing, who are the "least of these" in your community?
Around the world?

____

____

____

____

Read: Mark 2:1-12; Luke 8:43-48; John 9:1-7

Discuss: *Identify some of the lengths to which people went to receive Jesus' healing.*
Why do you think Jesus had some people complete various "tasks" in order to be healed?
Do you believe that Jesus is still about healing today? How?

____

____

____

____

Read: Acts 3:1-10; James 5:13-16

Discuss: *What was Peter's bold action?*
On whose authority did Peter proclaim healing?

What are believers called to do for those who are hurting or in need of healing?

Notes

____

____

____

____

When the small groups are finished, gather again as a large group and share insights.

Closing

As you end your ministry team meeting, gather in a circle for prayers of the people. Select someone to begin the prayer and someone to close the prayer. During the prayer, each person should lift up a prayer for healing or for the work of your ministry team. Respond to each prayer by saying together, "Lord, in your mercy, hear our prayer."

Homework and Business

If you haven't already, you may want to select a leader to facilitate your group meetings. It may also be helpful to have a secretary who can help the group stay informed about projects you'll take on.

For your next meeting, you'll want to read through Session Two: Together In Ministry Everyday. Be prepared to discuss your homework. Don't worry though—you won't be graded on your performance!

Session Two:
Together in Ministry Everyday

Prepare for your next group meeting by working through the T.I.M.E. outline. Pray through the questions and make notes that you can share with the group.

Notes

Opening

Gather as a community and open with prayer. Choose a volunteer to lead a prayer or pray together the following corporate prayer:

"Healing God, we are here to put our whole selves into healing your sheep. Ignite a passion in us to bring healing and compassion to our community and to our world. Equip us to do your healing work. In the name of Christ we pray, amen."

Storytelling

Discuss where you've seen moments of healing since your last group meeting. If you need to, use the following questions to prompt discussion:

- *How have you seen God at work through healing lately?*
- *In what ways have you personally experienced God's healing through the love and compassion of another person?*

Notes

T.I.M.E.

Before your meeting, work through these questions and be prepared to discuss your answers. For your group meeting, depending on the size of your group, you may want to divide into smaller groups to talk about your answers to these questions.

T

Take a look around.

- Take off your blinders and ask yourself: am I ignoring people and situations that need healing? What do I know about persons and situations in need of healing?
- What is your congregation currently doing to bring about healing? What improvements could be made?

- What connections exist within your congregation? Do you have networks with any community or global healing ministries?

I

Identify and investigate.

Where is there a need for healing?

Who are the contacts with whom our group should connect?

Notes

What do these contacts need from us in order for our group to connect with their mission?

____

____

M

Meditate and motivate.

- How is God speaking to me about my role in a healing ministry?

____

____

____

____

- What does my heart tell me?

____

____

____

____

- How can I make a difference?

____

____

____

____

E

Embrace and encourage.

- I'm ready to roll up my sleeves and get started. Mother Teresa said, *"There are no great things, only small things with great love."* Name three small things you can do with great love in the area of healing.

____

____

____

____

Notes

- How can you live out your faith through this work? What kind of impact might your faith work have on you? On others around you?

____

____

____

____

- How might your work on a healing ministry team reflect on the mission and vision of your church?

____

____

____

____

If you divided into smaller groups, gather the large group together and share any highlights from your conversations.

Closing

As you end your ministry team meeting, gather in a circle for prayers of the people. Select someone to begin the prayer and someone to close the prayer. During the prayer, each person should lift up a prayer for healing or for the work of your ministry team. Respond to each prayer by saying together, "Lord, in your mercy, hear our prayer."

Homework/Business

Session three is a planning meeting. Determine how to begin your work and what the needs and various roles might be. Assign tasks and research that will be discussed at your next ministry team meeting. Plan to create a plan for action at your next meeting.

Session Three:
Putting Plans into Action

Notes

Opening

Gather as a community and open with prayer. Choose a volunteer to lead a prayer or pray together the following corporate prayer:

"Healing God, we are here to put our whole selves into healing your sheep. Ignite a passion in us to bring healing and compassion to our community and to our world. Equip us to do your healing work. In the name of Christ we pray, amen."

Storytelling

Discuss where you've seen moments of healing since your last group meeting. If you need to, use the following questions to prompt discussion:

- *How have you seen God at work through healing lately?*
- *In what ways have you personally experienced God's healing through the love and compassion of another person?*
- *Where do you see a need for healing in the world?*

Inspiration

View the DVD segment, "Heal My Sheep." Then, discuss the following questions.

- *What spoke the loudest to you in the video?*
- *Did anything make your heart leap?*
- *How can your group join in local and global health initiatives to bring God's healing to the world?*

Notes

Planning

What are your plans for a healing ministry?

____

____

____

____

____

____

How would describe your work to others in your congregation in order to invite them to join you?

____

____

____

____

What needs to be done and who will do the work?

____

____

____

____

____

____

____

____

Closing

As you end your ministry team meeting, gather in a circle for prayers of the people. Select someone to begin the prayer and someone to close the prayer. During the prayer, each person should lift up a prayer for healing or for the work of your ministry team. Respond to each prayer by saying together, "Lord, in your mercy, hear our prayer."

Benediction

Notes

Read aloud the benediction and then "go and do likewise."

"May the God of healing fill our hearts and minds with courage, conviction, compassion, and love as we seek to heal God's lambs in this world. May we feel the power of the Holy Spirit in our actions and share the love of Christ with everyone we meet. Amen."

Chapter Four
Hug My Sheep

"A hug is like a boomerang—you get it back right away."
—Bill Keane, "Family Circus"

"A hug is the shortest distance between friends."
—Author unknown

"HIV does not make people dangerous to know, so you can shake their hands and give them a hug: Heaven knows they need it."
—Princess Diana

"If you hug to yourself any resentment against anybody else, you destroy the bridge by which God would come to you."
—Rev. Dr. Peter Marshall

Session One: **Wrap Your Arms Around the World**
Session Two: **Together in Ministry Everyday**
Session Three: **Putting Plans into Action**

Session One:
Wrap Your Arms Around the World

Notes

Opening

Gather as a community and open with prayer. Choose a volunteer to lead a prayer or pray together the following corporate prayer:

"Compassionate God, we are here to put our whole selves into hugging your sheep. Ignite a passion in us to bring comfort to and share your peace in our community and our world. Equip us to do your compassionate work. In the name of Christ we pray, amen."

Devotion

Take turns reading aloud the essay *"I Need a Hug!"*

I Need a Hug!

How many times have you walked up to a friend and said, "I need a hug!"? Hugging is an epidemic, and no one wants a cure. Consider that no government funding has ever been sought for the eradication of hugging. Just look at all of the bumper stickers that mention the greatness of the hug: "Have You Hugged a Child Today?," "Hug a Soldier," "Hug a Teacher," "Hug a Tree," "Hug a Logger. You'll Never Go Back to Trees," "A Hug Is the Ideal Gift – One Size Fits All."

Everybody loves hugs. Children love hugs—in fact, hugs may be the last refuge of parents of teenagers whose children

Notes

have banned any other form of emotional contact other than gifts of cash. Women love hugs. Hugs are even widely accepted as a public display of affection for men; throw in a good pat on the back for extra emphasis.

Hugging is universal. It has no need for an interpreter. Even groups hug! Know what that little thingy is called that you put around your soda can to keep your drink cold? Yep. A huggie. Hugs say, "I come in peace," "I care about you," and "Welcome home, I'm double parked in the white zone, let's get your bags and go!"

What is the deal with hugs? Why do they have such a universal effect? Why are they so healing? Why do we need them? Turns out, the reason might have something to do with how the human body is engineered. Of the five senses—sight, smell, hearing, taste, and touch—touch is our oldest, most primitive and pervasive sense. Touch is the first sense we experience in the womb and the last one we lose before death. And our skin, which has about 50 touch receptors for every square centimeter and about five million sensory cells overall, loves to be touched.

Our other four senses are located in specific parts of the body, but our sense of touch is found all over our bodies in our nerve-ending receptors. These receptors send messages directly to our brains and, unlike most cell phone towers, the signal is received loud and clear. Those feelings are registered by our brain. Hugs are good feelings, warm feelings, happy feelings.

Unfortunately, our bodies register pain as well as pleasure. Is it any wonder, then, that we crave hugs to balance out the pain in our lives? The need for compassionate, loving, physical contact is borne out best in the example of orphans. Babies who are not held do not thrive. Their capacity to learn is

Notes

significantly diminished. They do not grow at the rate of babies who are given loving attention. Saddest of all, after a period of time they stop crying for attention, because attention never comes.

In Africa, babies born with HIV, or suspected of being born with HIV, are abandoned by their mothers. There are many reasons: stigma, poverty, fear, a sick mother who cannot care even for herself. The chances of a baby with HIV being adopted in Africa are virtually nonexistent.

I was in Eldoret, Kenya in 2004 with a team making a documentary about the life-changing work of the IU/Kenya partnership in the field of treating HIV/AIDS. As the writer, it was my job to interview, observe, and take notes. On the day that we toured the pediatric ward of the hospital, however, I threw down my notebook and pen in order to hold Esther. Writing could wait. My body had a far more important task at hand.

Esther was abandoned in the dirty city markets of Eldoret when she was days old. She was still only a few weeks old when I saw her, and I knew that she needed the rare, undivided attention that I could afford to give her. There are far too many children for the staff to do much more than keep up with their basic needs. Long periods of time being held, rocked, and talked to are rare.

For as long as I could, I held Esther and talked to her. An infant's need to suckle is incredible, so when I offered up my pinky she took it eagerly. When her formula was finally warmed, I fed her with a syringe; bottles were not available.

I was not able to change the course of Esther's life with the short time I spent with her, but I know I gave her something she desperately needed—something we all need, especially in

Notes

times of pain and sadness. I gave her my loving arms, my time, my acceptance, my compassion.

Close your eyes and visualize the act of preparing to hug someone else. What's the most necessary component? You must have your arms wide open. You cannot hug someone else with your arms hanging limply at your side, or wrapped around yourself. You have to be open in order to be caring.

Are your arms wide open? Are you ready to give compassionate, inclusive, loving, Christ-like care to those who are hurting? Hugs are simply a metaphor for being a conduit of God's love through the simple act of being compassionately available—to reaching out when family, friends, colleagues, friends, or strangers need us. Blanche DuBois isn't the only one who has always depended on the kindness of strangers. We all have. So stretch your arms wide, take a deep breath, and get ready to give the world a hug.

Storytelling

Take a few minutes to share personal hug stories. You may also want to share any insights you gained from the Hug My Sheep chapter in the T.I.M.E. Handbook. Here are some questions to guide your discussion:

- *Describe the best hug you've ever received.*
- *Why do you think you are feeling led to participate in compassion ministries?*
- *What is your dream for the compassion ministry in your church?*

Bible Study

Divide into small groups to read the following Scriptures and discuss the questions.

Notes

Read: Luke 15:1-7

Discuss: *What do we learn about compassion in this Scripture passage?*
Where do you find yourself among the characters? The accuser? The lost sheep? The shepherd?
What does it feel like to be "found" when you're lost?

____

____

____

____

Read: Luke 15:11-32

Discuss: *Where does compassion find its way into this story?*
Describe the emotions of both the father and the lost son as they hugged upon his return home.
How easy is it to act like the brother? Why?
What are the implications for a compassion outreach ministry in our church?

____

____

____

____

Read: John 11:28-37

Discuss: *Why is it so comforting to know that Jesus wept over the death of his friend?*
What are the various emotions experienced by those in the Scripture passage?
Where are the moments of compassion?

____

____

____

____

Notes

Read: John 14:1-3, 18-31

Discuss: *Describe the tone Jesus uses in these sections of Scripture.*

Why do you think Jesus is concerned with comforting his disciples?

How can your group be one that speaks peace into uneasy situations?

____

____

____

____

When the small groups are finished, gather again as a large group and share insights.

Closing

As you end your ministry team meeting, gather in a circle for prayers of the people. Select someone to begin the prayer and someone to close the prayer. During the prayer, each person should lift up a prayer for the work of your ministry team. Respond to each prayer by saying together, "Lord, in your mercy, hear our prayer."

Homework and Business

If you haven't already, you may want to select a leader to facilitate your group meetings. It may also be helpful to have a secretary who can help the group stay informed about projects you'll take on.

For your next meeting, you'll want to read through Session Two: Together in Ministry Everyday. Be prepared to discuss your homework. Don't worry though—you won't be graded on your performance!

Session Two:
Together in Ministry Everyday

Prepare for your next group meeting by working through the T.I.M.E. outline. Pray through the questions and make notes that you can share with the group.

Notes

Opening

Gather as a community and open with prayer. Choose a volunteer to lead a prayer or pray together the following corporate prayer:

"Compassionate God, we are here to put our whole selves into hugging your sheep. Ignite a passion in us to bring comfort to and share your peace in our community and our world. Equip us to do your compassionate work. In the name of Christ we pray, amen."

Storytelling

Discuss where you've seen moments of compassion since your last group meeting. If you need to, use the following questions to prompt discussion:

- *How have you seen God at work through compassionate people?*
- *In what ways have you personally experienced a hug from God?*

Notes

T.I.M.E.

Before your meeting, work through these questions and be prepared to discuss your answers. For your group meeting, depending on the size of your group, you may want to divide into smaller groups to talk about your answers to these questions.

T

Take a look around.

- Take off your blinders and ask yourself: am I ignoring people and situations that need a compassionate hug? What do I know about persons and situations in need of compassion and comfort?
- What is your congregation currently doing to bring hugs to your community? What improvements could be made?

- What connections exist within your congregation? Do you have networks with any community or global compassion ministries?

I

Identify and investigate.

- Where is there a need for a hug?

Notes

- Who are the contacts with whom our group should connect?

- What do these contacts need from us in order for our group to connect with their mission?

M

Meditate and motivate.

- How is God speaking to me about my role in a compassion ministry?

- What does my heart tell me?

- How can I make a difference?

E

Embrace and encourage.

- I'm ready to roll up my sleeves and get started. Mother Teresa said, *"There are no great things, only small things*

Notes

with great love." Name three small things you can do with great love in the area of compassion.

___

___

___

___

- How can you live out your faith through this work? What kind of impact might your faith work have on you? On others around you?
- How might your work on a compassion ministry team reflect on the mission and vision of your church?

___

___

___

___

If you divided into smaller groups, gather the large group together and share any highlights from your conversations.

Closing

As you end your ministry team meeting, gather in a circle for prayers of the people. Select someone to begin the prayer and someone to close the prayer. During the prayer, each person should lift up a prayer for the work of your ministry team. Respond to each prayer by saying together, "Lord, in your mercy, hear our prayer."

Homework/Business

Session three is a planning meeting. Determine how to begin your work and what the needs and various roles might be. Assign tasks and research that will be discussed at your next ministry team meeting. Plan to create a plan for action at your next meeting.

Session Three:
Putting Plans into Action

Opening

Notes

Gather as a community and open with prayer. Choose a volunteer to lead a prayer or pray together the following corporate prayer:

"Compassionate God, we are here to put our whole selves into hugging your sheep. Ignite a passion in us to bring comfort to and share your peace in our community and our world. Equip us to do your compassionate work. In the name of Christ we pray, amen."

Storytelling

Discuss where you've seen moments of compassion since your last group meeting. If you need to, use the following questions to prompt discussion:

- *How have you seen God at work through compassionate acts lately?*
- *In what ways have you personally experienced a hug from God through the love and compassion of another person?*
- *Where do you see a need for hugs in the world?*

Inspiration

View the DVD segment, "Hug My Sheep." Then, discuss the following questions.

Notes

- *What spoke the loudest to you in the video?*

- *Did anything make your heart leap?*

- *How can your group join in local and global compassion ministries to bring a hug from God to the world?*

Planning

What are your plans for a compassion ministry?

How would describe your work to others in your congregation in order to invite them to join you?

What needs to be done and who will do the work?

Closing

As you end your ministry team meeting, gather in a circle for prayers of the people. Select someone to begin the prayer and

Notes

someone to close the prayer. During the prayer, each person should lift up a prayer for the work of your ministry team. Respond to each prayer by saying together, "Lord, in your mercy, hear our prayer."

Benediction

Read aloud the benediction and then "go and do likewise."

"May God fill our hearts with compassion and a desire to bring comfort and peace in uncomfortable and uneasy situations. May the God who has the whole world in God's hands extend the reach of our arms as we seek to wrap our arms around the world. Through Christ our Lord, we pray, amen."

Chapter Five
Shelter My Sheep

"Oh, a storm is threatening
My very life today
If I don't get some shelter
I'm gonna fade away"
—"Gimme Shelter" by The Rolling Stones

Session One: **We Need a Refuge**
Session Two: **Together in Ministry Everyday**
Session Three: **Putting Plans into Action**

Session One:
We Need a Refuge

Opening

Notes

Gather as a community and open with prayer. Choose a volunteer to lead a prayer or pray together the following corporate prayer:

"God, we are here to put our whole selves into sheltering your sheep. Show us what you desire for our work and give us the courage and wisdom to say yes. Amen."

Devotion

Take turns reading aloud the essay, "*Give Me Shelter.*"

Give Me Shelter

"Seek shelter immediately!"

Those are the words uttered by all TV meteorologists as they alert the public to the potential of serious storms. When those life-threatening storms approach, over and over we are told to seek shelter. We are not told to gather our personal belongings. We are not told to prepare a large meal. We are not told to backup our computer files. We are told in no uncertain terms to seek shelter.

Most of us are fortunate to have shelter when the storms of life hit. We have a home. We have insurance. We have

Notes

family, friends, faith. What would it feel like to have no shelter? No physical shelter, or no emotional shelter, or both? A turtle with its shell is nearly invincible; without its shell it is vulnerable to everything. Without shelter we are vulnerable to everything. Homelessness, poverty, disease, and depression prey on those who have lost their shelter.

In the movie *Castaway*, Tom Hanks portrays Chuck Noland, a Fed Ex employee. While on a business trip, the Fed Ex plane on which he was flying encountered a raging thunderstorm that threw them hundreds of miles off course somewhere in the South Pacific. The plane crashed in flames into the sea. Chuck is the sole survivor of the crash. He washes up on the shore of a deserted island with only a raft, the clothes that managed to stay on his back, and a pocket watch given to him by his beloved fiancée, a picture of her inside the cover.

Chuck's first mission after coming to grips with his situation is clear: finding water and creating shelter. He manages to craft a rudimentary lean-to with sticks and his raft that provides some protection but is of little help during raging storms. As he gets to know the island better, he discovers a small cave which provides more protection from the unrelenting rain.

After a few days, Fed Ex packages from the plane begin to wash up on shore. At first, Chuck simply tosses them into a pile. After frustrated attempts to create fire, however, Chuck decides to start opening the packages. Chuck finds new purposes for the treasures these packages contain. Videotapes become lashings. A fancy dress provides netting for catching fish. A pair of ice skates become blades for cutting, chopping, and providing flint for making much-needed fire. And a Wilson volleyball becomes his best friend, providing emotional shelter.

Notes

While trying to create fire, Chuck cuts his hand with the ice skate blade. Frustrated, angry and in pain, he grabs the stark white volleyball and hurls it with his bloody hand, leaving an imprint. Feeling bad that he threw the ball, Chuck goes to retrieve it. Seeing the imprint, he creates facial features in the palm area of his handprint, the fingerprints serving as the hair. He calls him Wilson, after the manufacturer of the ball.

Over the course of four years on the island, Chuck becomes an adept fisherman and survivalist. Wilson becomes Chuck's fast friend and confidant. They have "conversations" during which they process decisions, argue and share thoughts, including a dialogue about Chuck's attempted suicide attempt a year earlier.

Eventually, Chuck is able to construct a raft that is seaworthy enough to withstand the strong waves surrounding the island. With Wilson tethered to the front of the raft, they are adrift at sea. Chuck looks back emotionally at the island that was his home, his shelter for four years, but knows he must leave. And he still has Wilson, so he is not alone.

As Chuck is sleeping and adrift at sea, waves and parts of the raft work on Wilson's tether ropes, and he falls off the raft. When Chuck awakes and sees that Wilson is no longer there, he calls out for him. Desperate, he dives into the ocean, searching for him, crying out Wilson's name, but to no avail. In a truly emotional scene, Chuck climbs back onto the raft, sobbing inconsolably for the loss of his friend.

In this movie we see our primal need for shelter laid bare. Of course we all think of shelter in terms of housing or protection. A drop of rain, and we turn to portable shelter: umbrellas, a newspaper, a small awning.

But look at the lengths to which the character Chuck went

Notes

for emotional shelter. During times of great distress, it was a need that had to be met in order for him to survive. Chuck needed a friend. He needed someone to talk to, someone to bounce ideas off of, someone to encourage him, argue with him, comfort him with his presence by simply being there.

There are many people trying to survive in this world. Truly, day-to-day survival. They have no shelter of job or income. They have no protection against abuse. The safety of family has fallen in around them. Tragically, many people feel forced to take any port in a storm when they are lacking shelter. They feel alone and helpless. They need help. No matter the specifics of their needs, they first need the sheltering presence of God's love through our acts. If a volleyball can provide emotional shelter for one castaway, think how much more your care and concern can do for a person in need.

The Rolling Stones sing, "Oh, a storm is threatening my very life today. If I don't get some shelter, I'm gonna fade away." The storms of life are threatening millions of people in our world today. They need a resurrection, a fresh start. Because the stone was rolled away, because of the living example of Jesus, we know what we are called to do.

If you Google the word *shelter*, you will find that you get about 64,500,000 entries. If you Google the word *god*, you'll get about 639,000,000. Googling *love* renders a whopping 2,270,000,000. To put this in perspective, *pizza* turns up 208,000,000, and *anchovies* 1,730,000.

This highly scientific polling strategy would seem to validate what we know: the world seeks love, God, and shelter. Love and God outrank pizza. Pizza outranks shelter, but we all know a good pizza makes life better one slice at a time. As for anchovies–well, enough said.

Notes

So order up a big ole cheesy pizza pie, get a volleyball for inspiration, dig in and ask yourself: how can I follow the example set by a carpenter over two thousand years ago and go about the business of building shelters for those who need them most?

Storytelling

Take a few minutes to share personal stories about needing shelter. You may also want to share any insights you gained from the Shelter My Sheep chapter in the T.I.M.E. Handbook. Here are some questions to guide your discussion:

- *In what ways have you experienced or witnessed a need for shelter?*
- *Why do you think you are feeling led to participate in a ministry of shelter?*
- *What is your dream for a ministry in your church that provides shelter?*

Bible Study

Divide into small groups to read the following Scriptures and discuss the questions.

Read: Deuteronomy 10:17-19

Discuss: *What does it mean to care for the orphan and the widow in today's context?*
What does it mean to love the stranger today?
How can we worship God by loving and caring for the stranger, orphan, and widow?

____

____

____

____

Notes

Read: Psalm 61:1-4

Discuss: *What does it mean that God is our "refuge"?*
Describe what comes to mind when you imagine "abiding in God's tent" and "finding refuge in the shelter of [God's] wings."

____

____

____

____

Read: Matthew 25:40-46

Discuss: *Why is Jesus so harsh with those who did not care for the "least of these?"*
How can we welcome the stranger?
What are the implications for us as we plan for a new ministry of shelter?

____

____

____

____

Read: Luke 6:46-48

Discuss: *What does it mean to build a house on rock?*
How can we be a ministry built on a firm foundation?
How can we point to God as our foundation as we seek to bring shelter?

____

____

____

____

When the small groups are finished, gather again as a large group and share insights.

Closing

Notes

As you end your ministry team meeting, gather in a circle for prayers of the people. Select someone to begin the prayer and someone to close the prayer. During the prayer, each person should lift up a prayer for the work of your ministry team. Respond to each prayer by saying together, "Lord, in your mercy, hear our prayer."

Homework and Business

If you haven't already, you may want to select a leader to facilitate your group meetings. It may also be helpful to have a secretary who can help the group stay informed about projects you'll take on.

For your next meeting, you'll want to read through Session Two: Together in Ministry Everyday. Be prepared to discuss your homework. Don't worry though—you won't be graded on your performance!

Session Two:
Together in Ministry Everyday

Prepare for your next group meeting by working through the T.I.M.E. outline. Pray through the questions and make notes that you can share with the group.

Notes

Opening
Gather as a community and open with prayer. Choose a volunteer to lead a prayer or pray together the following corporate prayer:

"God, we are here to put our whole selves into sheltering your sheep. Show us what you desire for our work and give us the courage and wisdom to say yes. Amen."

Storytelling
Discuss where you've experienced shelter since your last group meeting. If you need to, use the following questions to prompt discussion:

- *How have you seen lives change by finding shelter?*
- *In what ways have you personally experienced refuge under God's shelter?*

T.I.M.E.
Before your meeting, work through these questions and be prepared to discuss your answers. For your group meeting,

Notes

depending on the size of your group, you may want to divide into smaller groups to talk about your answers to these questions.

T

Take a look around.

- Take off your blinders and ask yourself: Am I ignoring people and situations that need shelter? What do I know about persons and situations in need of shelter?

____

____

____

____

- What is your congregation currently doing to provide shelter? What improvements could be made?

____

____

____

____

- What connections exist within your congregation? Do you have networks with any community or global housing ministries?

____

____

____

____

I

Identify and investigate.

- Where is there a need for shelter?

____

____

Notes

- Who are the contacts with whom our group should connect?

- What do these contacts need from us in order for our group to connect with their mission?

Meditate and motivate.

M

- How is God speaking to me about my role in a ministry of providing shelter?

- What does my heart tell me?

- How can I make a difference?

Embrace and encourage.

E

- I'm ready to roll up my sleeves and get started. Mother Teresa said, *"There are no great things, only small things with great love."* Name three small things you can do with great love in the area of providing shelter.

Notes

- How can you live out your faith through this work? What kind of impact might your faith work have on you? On others around you?

- How might your work on a shelter ministry team reflect on the mission and vision of your church?

If you divided into smaller groups, gather the large group together and share any highlights from your conversations.

Closing

As you end your ministry team meeting, gather in a circle for prayers of the people. Select someone to begin the prayer and someone to close the prayer. During the prayer, each person should lift up a prayer for the work of your ministry team. Respond to each prayer by saying together, "Lord, in your mercy, hear our prayer."

Homework/Business

Session three is a planning meeting. Determine how to begin your work and what the needs and various roles might be. Assign tasks and research that will be discussed at your next ministry team meeting. Plan to create a plan for action at your next meeting.

Session Three:
Putting Plans into Action

Notes

Opening

Gather as a community and open with prayer. Choose a volunteer to lead a prayer or pray together the following corporate prayer:

"God, we are here to put our whole selves into sheltering your sheep. Show us what you desire for our work and give us the courage and wisdom to say yes. Amen."

Storytelling

Discuss where you've seen moments of healing since your last group meeting. If you need to, use the following questions to prompt discussion:

- *In what ways have you experienced or witnessed a need for shelter?*
- *Why do you think you are feeling led to participate in a ministry of shelter?*
- *What is your dream for a ministry that provides shelter in your church?*

Inspiration

View the DVD segment, "Shelter My Sheep." Then, discuss the following questions.

Notes

- *What spoke the loudest to you in the video?*

- *Did anything make your heart leap?*

- *How can your group share God's love by joining in local and global shelter ministries?*

Planning

What are your plans for a shelter ministry?

How would describe your work to others in your congregation in order to invite them to join you?

What needs to be done and who will do the work?

Notes

____

____

____

____

Closing

As you end your ministry team meeting, gather in a circle for prayers of the people. Select someone to begin the prayer and someone to close the prayer. During the prayer, each person should lift up a prayer for the work of your ministry team. Respond to each prayer by saying together, "Lord, in your mercy, hear our prayer."

Benediction

Read aloud the benediction and then "go and do likewise."

"May the God of Refuge who hides us in the shadow of God's wings give us courage and vision to begin a ministry of bringing shelter to those who need it most. May we feel the call and act as we welcome the stranger and help to spread the shelter of God's love in our community and in the world. Through Christ our Lord, we pray, amen."

T.I.M.E. Ministry Survey

Put an X beside the statement that feels most like your entry point into mission evangelism. Imagine where you find the most passion when it comes to reaching others with the love of God. Choose only one per question.

1.

__Thomas was a homeless man who ate breakfast at the rescue mission every morning. He is working to get back on his feet and needs a friend and advocate.

__The students at an inner-city school in your area have all but given up on hope. They would believe in possibility if someone showed an interest in their well-being.

__The HIV/AIDS pandemic in Africa is taking entirely too many lives. If clinics had the proper funding, staffing, and volunteer support more people would survive this disease.

__Cheri lost her job a month ago. Since then she has discovered that she has breast cancer. Her family is a support for her, but she is longing for a spiritual friend to lean on.

__When Hurricane Katrina hit the Gulf Coast, thousands of people lost their homes. The news showed the wreckage the storm left. They also showed volunteers working day and night to build new homes for victims of the storm.

2.

__Samantha and her two small children live happily in a rural, one bedroom apartment. The three of them are content no matter what life brings them, but Samantha works four jobs to pay the bills. Food gets cut first from the list. Samantha depends on the friendly volunteers at the local food bank to feed her children each month.

__A new inmate-education program just began where people can volunteer to help inmates complete their GED requirements so that they leave jail with a basic education.

__A group of people in a local church believed so strongly in the power of prayer that they began a healing prayer ministry. They seek out persons in need of healing and commit to prayer with those persons as long as they wish to receive them.

__The children's home in town is looking for mentors to partner with the children as advocates, tutors, and friends.

__The local Habitat for Humanity chapter has invited your church to work with them on three builds this year.

3.

__The Vacation Bible School kids are collecting food for your church's food pantry. They are looking for an adult to lead the mission effort and coordinate donations.

__Your church is right down the street from a school for children and adults with special needs. They have posted a need for tutors and volunteers.

__ Your pastor is starting weekly healing prayer services and needs people to commit to being present as prayer partners for people who might come.

__Overcrowded orphanages all over the world depend on people who are willing to travel and be part-time caregivers to babies. They are thrilled when people come and volunteer to hold and show love to infants who so desperately need to be loved.

__A building team is working to build wheelchair ramps and do handiwork for those who need it.

4.

__Your church has taken on the Food Stamp Challenge for the Lenten Season. Each family will shop and eat as though they received food stamps as an act of education and solidarity.

__ A teenager in your church had an idea of reaching out to the community by creating a computer center in the church building that students and others could use for homework, job searches, and educational activities. She also wants to hold various classes as an outreach.

__A free, non-profit pediatric medical clinic is holding a certified nurse assistant training in hopes of building their pool of volunteer nurse assistants.

__The pediatric medical clinic is also holding a teddy bear drive so each child that receives care will also receive a comforting teddy bear.

__A tornado demolished a town about an hour away. Rebuilding is slow, but they're taking all the volunteers they can get.

5.

__The youth director invited help for the 30 Hour Famine experience the youth will be participating in.

__A new believer's Bible study program is starting up and in need of small group leaders.

__Your church has begun a Nothing But Nets campaign to buy protective sleeping nets for children in Africa. The nets protect the children from malaria.

__ The juvenile detention center in town is asking for mentors to sit in group sessions to act as positive, adult, role models and advocates for the kids.

__A local ministry that helps women get out of prostitution and off the streets needs additional housing for the women. Their plan is to build a village of dorms, but they need volunteers to build them.

Assessment

If you checked mostly the first statement, then you probably find the most passion around hunger ministries. You connect to the idea that feeding bellies can also feed the soul and points people to God's love. You may want to re-read the Feed My Sheep chapter of the T.I.M.E. Handbook or join the Feed My Sheep ministry action team.

If you checked mostly the second statement, then you may have a strong leaning towards education ministries. You might see education as an entry point for someone to the love of God. You may want to re-read the Teach My Sheep chapter of the T.I.M.E. Handbook or join the Teach My Sheep ministry action team.

If you checked mostly the third statement, then you might have a strong desire to bring God's healing to others. You find joy in participating in the healing work of God and believe healing to be a way of sharing God's love. You may want to re-read the Heal My Sheep chapter of the T.I.M.E. Handbook or join the Heal My Sheep ministry action team.

If you checked mostly the fourth statement, then you might lean towards solidarity, comfort, and advocacy ministries. You believe that hugs are not insignificant when people need them most. You probably show God's love by acts of hospitality and by your generous spirit. You may want to re-read the Hug My Sheep chapter of the T.I.M.E. Handbook or join the Hug My Sheep ministry action team.

If you checked mostly the fifth statement, you probably like to build things. You believe that providing physical shelter conveys a message of God's lve and spiritual shelter to someone who needs it most. You may want to re-read the Shelter My Sheep chapter of the T.I.M.E. Handbook or join the Shelter My Sheep ministry action team.

T.I.M.E.
Dedication Service

Opening Prayer:

"Compassionate and Loving God, we come to you today with great anticipation of what you will do when a dedicated group of followers commits to serve and feed your sheep. We know that you do great and mighty works through your church and we pray that you will do a mighty work in us. May our gifts of service be used to share your love. May those who don't know you now come to know you by our actions and our love. May our church grow and thrive because outsiders find this place to be where they belong. Bring your kingdom through our work. Through Christ our Lord we pray, amen.

Scripture Readings:

John 21:17; Matthew 9:35; James 5:13-16; Luke 15:20; Luke 6:46-48

Suggested Songs of Praise:

Here I Am, Lord
Shout to the North
I'm Gonna Live So God Can Use Me

Testimonies:

Invite members of your ministry teams to tell about the work they will be doing. Encourage them to communicate their sense of call to the mission and what they hope to see and how they hope to grow.

Closing Litany:

One: Lord, we know that people are hungry.
All: We hear you say, "Feed my sheep."
One: Lord, we know that education can lead to freedom and liberation.
All: We hear you say, "Teach my sheep."
One: Lord, we know that you healed through the apostles.
All: We hear you say, "Heal my sheep."
One: Lord, we know that you are all-compassionate.
All: We hear you say, "Hug my sheep."
One: Lord, we know that you shelter us in the shadow of your wings.
All: Lord, we hear you say, "Shelter my sheep."
One: Lord, bless our efforts.
All: Lord, bless our efforts.
One: And, may your kingdom come on earth
All: As it is in Heaven, amen.

My Ministry Action Team Roster

Name

Phone Numbers/Email

Name

Phone Numbers/Email

Name

Phone Numbers/Email

Name

Phone Numbers/Email

Name

Phone Numbers/Email

Name

Phone Numbers/Email

My Ministry Action Team Roster

Name

Phone Numbers/Email

Name

Phone Numbers/Email

Name

Phone Numbers/Email

Name

Phone Numbers/Email

Name

Phone Numbers/Email

Name

Phone Numbers/Email

Name

Phone Numbers/Email

My Ministry Action Team Roster

Name

Phone Numbers/Email

Name

Phone Numbers/Email

Name

Phone Numbers/Email

Name

Phone Numbers/Email

Name

Phone Numbers/Email

Name

Phone Numbers/Email

Name

Phone Numbers/Email
